# families

# families

Text by Debbie Bailey
Photographs by Susan Huszar

Annick Press Ltd.
Toronto • New York • Vancouver

We acknowledge the support of the Canada Council for the Arts for our publishing program.
We also thank the Ontario Arts Council.

We acknowledge the financial support of the Government of Canada through the Book
Publishing Industry Development Program for our publishing activities.

**Cataloguing in Publication Data**

Bailey, Debbie, 1954-
Families

Contents: My mom – My dad – Brothers – Sisters – Grandma – Grandpa.
ISBN 1-55037-594-6

1. Family – Juvenile literature. I. Huszar, Susan, 1955-  . II. Title

HQ744.B335 1999    j306.85    C99-930207-8

Distributed in Canada by:
Firefly Books Ltd.
3680 Victoria Park Avenue
Willowdale, ON
M2H 3K1

Published in the U.S.A. by:
Annick Press (U.S.) Ltd.
Distributed in the U.S.A. by:
Firefly Books (U.S.) Inc.
P.O. Box 1338, Ellicott Station
Buffalo, NY 14205

Printed and bound in Canada by
Metropole, Montréal, Québec.

Thanks to Rick and the staff at Annick.

—D.B.

To David, Karen, Kira and Callum.

—S.H.

MY MOM

My mom is very special.

We do lots of things together.

My mom plays with me.

We play music together,

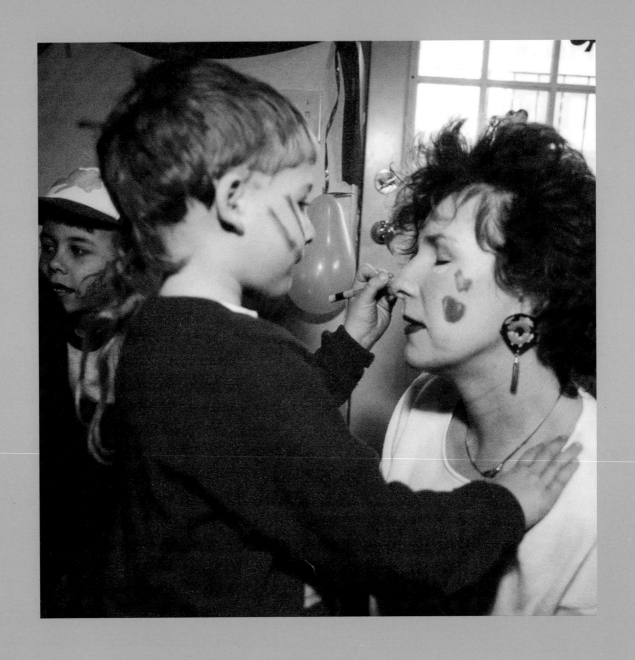

and paint funny faces on
each other.

My mom lets me do things
for myself,

but she helps me when I
need it.

I like to help my mom.
Sometimes we make supper.

My mom and I like to go
outside together.

She pushes me on the swing.

If I hurt myself, my mom
hugs me and I feel better.

I love my mom

and my mom loves me.

My mom!

# MY DAD

My dad is very special.

We play with toys,

and look at books.

My dad and I like to go
for walks.

Sometimes we walk to
the park

or go for an ice cream.

I like to help my dad
buy groceries.

When we cook together,

I set the table.

At the end of the day, my
dad gives me a bath,

and helps me comb my hair.

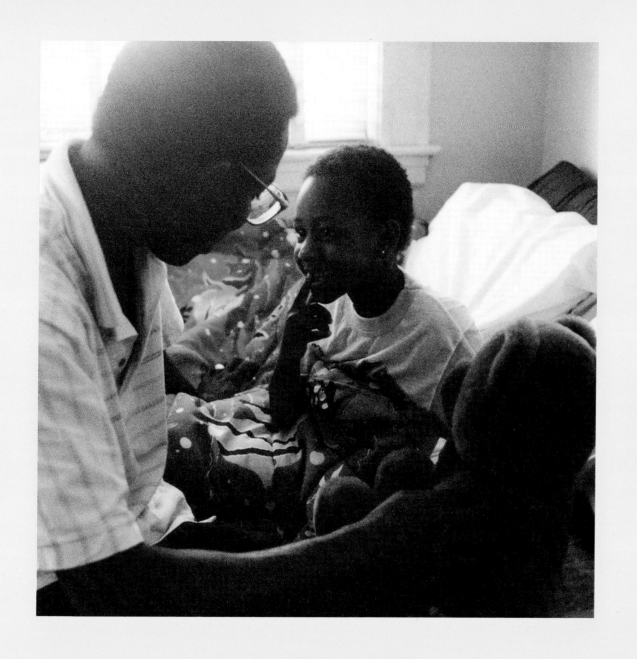

I love my dad

and my dad loves me.

My dad!

# BROTHERS

In some families there are brothers.

There may be lots of brothers,

two,

or only one.
Do you have a brother?

My brother is my friend.

We like to make each other
laugh.

I like to help my brother

and share things with him.

We like to do puzzles,

play outside,

pretend,

or just be together.

I wish everyone had a brother
like mine.

Brothers!

# SiSTERS

In some families there are sisters.

Some sisters are older,

some are younger,

and some are the same age.
Are you someone's sister?

Sisters are fun to do things with.

My sister and I like to play in
the sand,

have a party,

build things,

or dress up and pretend.

Sometimes we're noisy together,

and sometimes we're quiet.

I like it best when we tell each
other stories.

I wish everyone had a sister
like mine.

Sisters!

# GRANDPA

I love my grandpa.

He's always glad to see me.

I draw my best pictures for
Grandpa,

and sometimes bring him
flowers.

My grandpa and I have lots of
interesting talks.

He tells me stories about my
mom when she was little,

and I show him how to make things.

Grandpa and I like to go out together.

We go for a swim

or go tobogganing in winter.

When we're at home, we play games

or quietly read.

What do you like to do with
your grandpa?

Grandpa!

# GRANDMA

I love my grandma.

We have fun together.

Sometimes we're together with
our family,

and sometimes it's just Grandma
and me.

When I'm with Grandma, we
talk about lots of things.

We go for walks,

and visit interesting places.

I like it when we take the bus!

Grandma and I like to help each other.

We build our own toys,

or work in the garden.

Grandma says I'm a big help.

What do you like to do with
your grandma?

Grandma!

The titles in this volume were originally published individually, in board-book format, as part of the *Talk-About-Books* series. The complete *Talk-About-Books* series includes:

*Toys*
*Hats*
*Shoes*
*Clothes*
*My Mom*
*My Dad*
*Sisters*
*Brothers*
*Grandma*
*Grandpa*
*My Family*
*The Playground*
*Let's Pretend*
*Happy Birthday*